AF364766

Text copyright © 2013 **Carmen Martínez Jover**
www.carmenmartinezjover.com
Illustrations copyright © 2014 **Rosemary Martínez**
www.rosemarymartinez.com

ISBN:978-607-29-3470-2

Forever Together, a single Mum by choice story.
1st edition November 2019

Forever Together, a single Mum by choice story with egg and sperm donation.
1st edition May 2022

Written by: Carmen Martínez Jover
Illustrated by: Rosemary Martínez
Collaborators: Victor Nieto, Abelardo & Mary Carmen Zepeda

Order your personalized edition with your family names:
https://books.carmenmartinezjover.com

I dedicate this story
with all my admiration to all
those single Mums by choice
who dance with love to the
daily rhythm of life to bring up
their children.

Carmen

Dedicated to all those
who dare to strive
for their dreams.

Rosemary

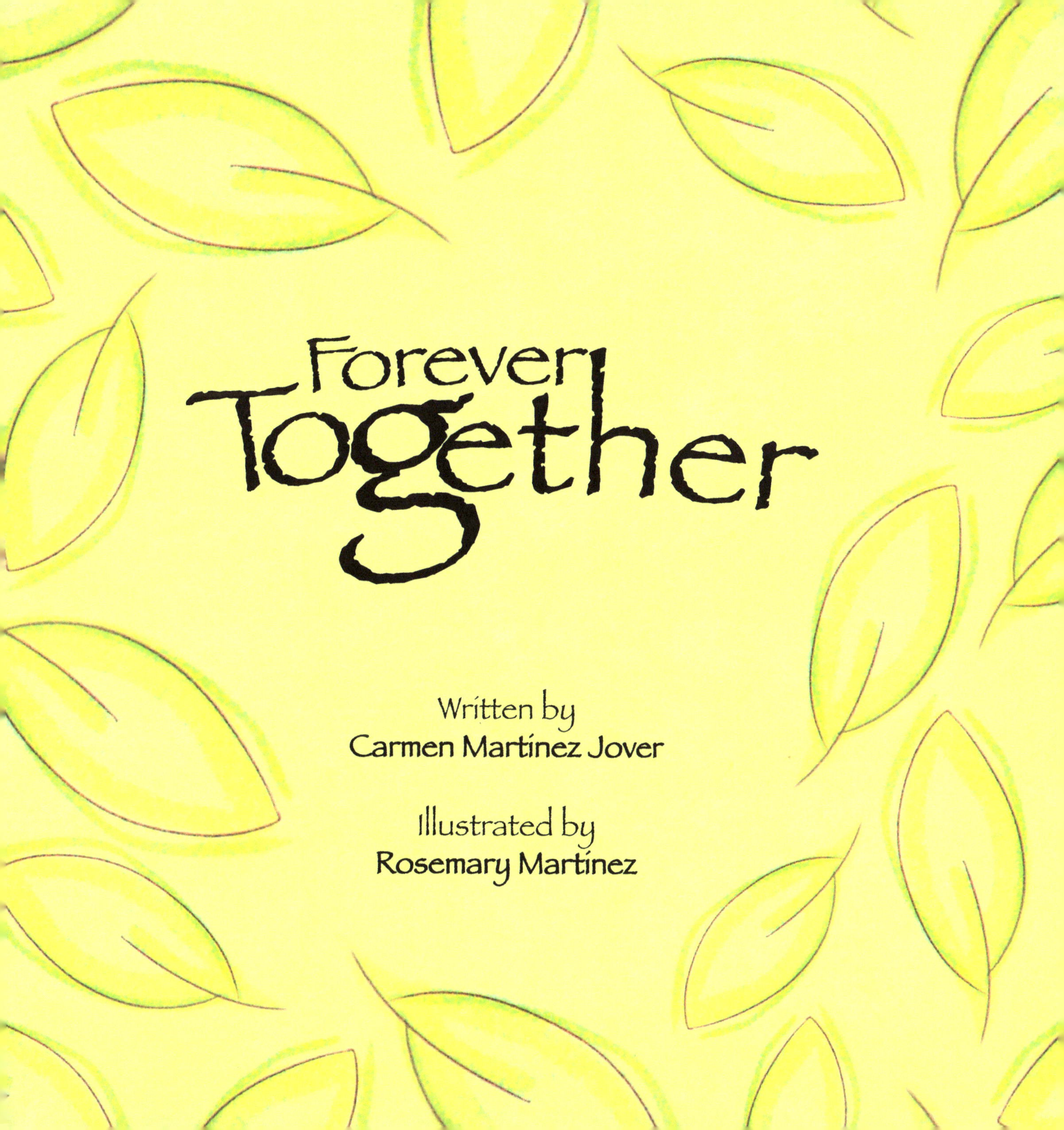

Forever Together

Written by
Carmen Martínez Jover

Illustrated by
Rosemary Martínez

Once upon a time there was a clever and friendly squirrel called Somy. She was named after Somilge, the Goddess of Magic.

She lived in a cosy tree which she had decorated to her taste.

7

Somy loved children and
she wanted to have one
of her own.

One evening, as Somy and
her neighbour Doris,
were tidying the house
after celebrating Somy's
birthday, Somy said:

"I'm getting older, Doris, and
I really want to have my own
baby squirrel. I feel time is
catching up on me."

11

So Somy started
looking for this
special person and
she met:

Huggy Hedgehog
and
Charming Chihuahua...

13

and
Geeky Goose

and
Funny Fox...

15

"Oh Doris, I'm so tired, I met lots
of possible partners but none of
them have conquered my heart.
And not one that I thought could
be a good Dad either,"
said Somy.

"I am worried, Doris, I feel that
I am growing too old to have
a baby, and that if I wait any
longer then I might never
be able to have a child."

"Well," said Doris, "you're right,
as time goes by your eggs and
womb get older and the chances
of you falling pregnant get smaller.

17

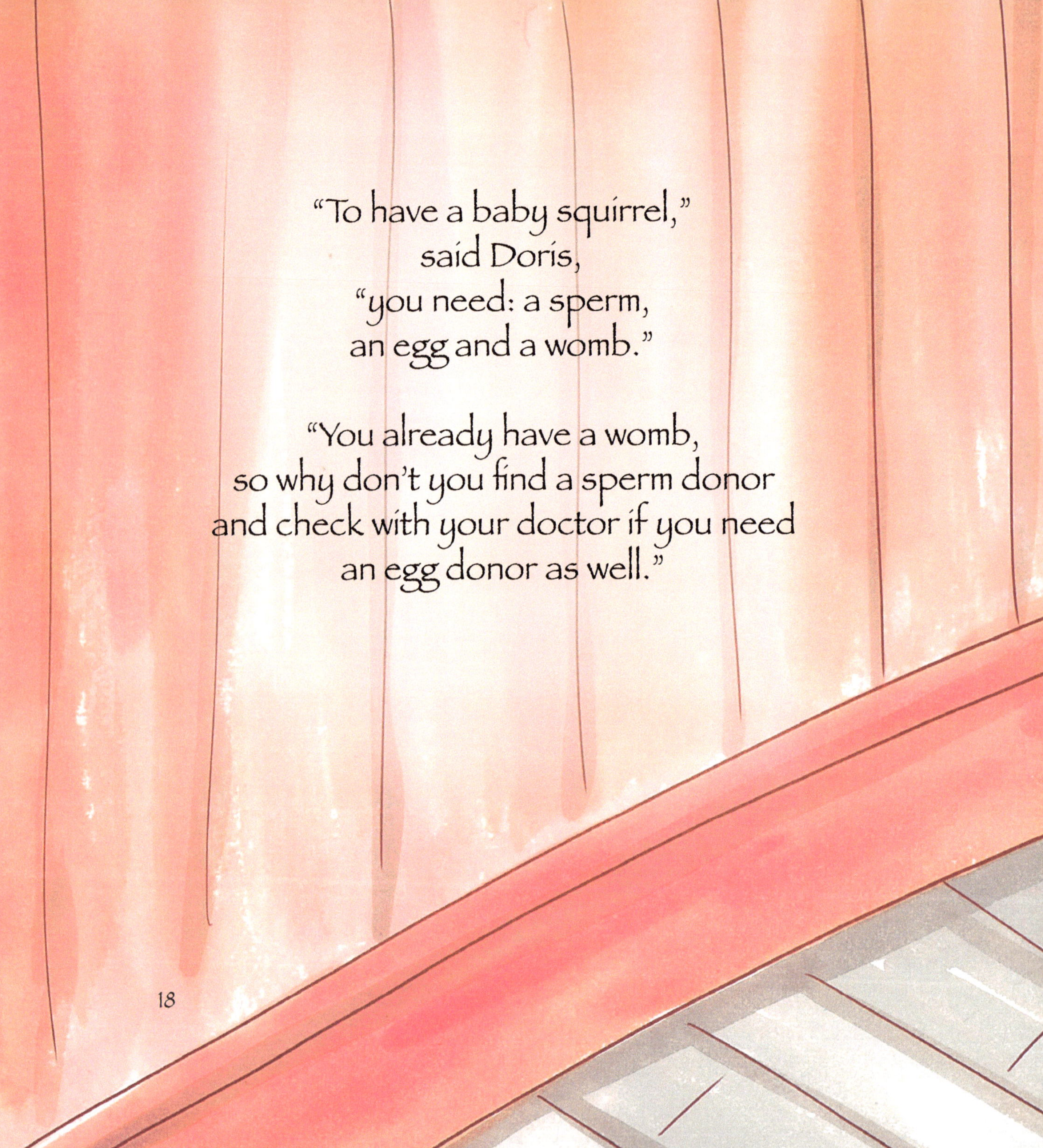
"To have a baby squirrel,"
said Doris,
"you need: a sperm,
an egg and a womb."

"You already have a womb,
so why don't you find a sperm donor
and check with your doctor if you need
an egg donor as well."

18

a sperm
an egg
a womb
a baby squirrel

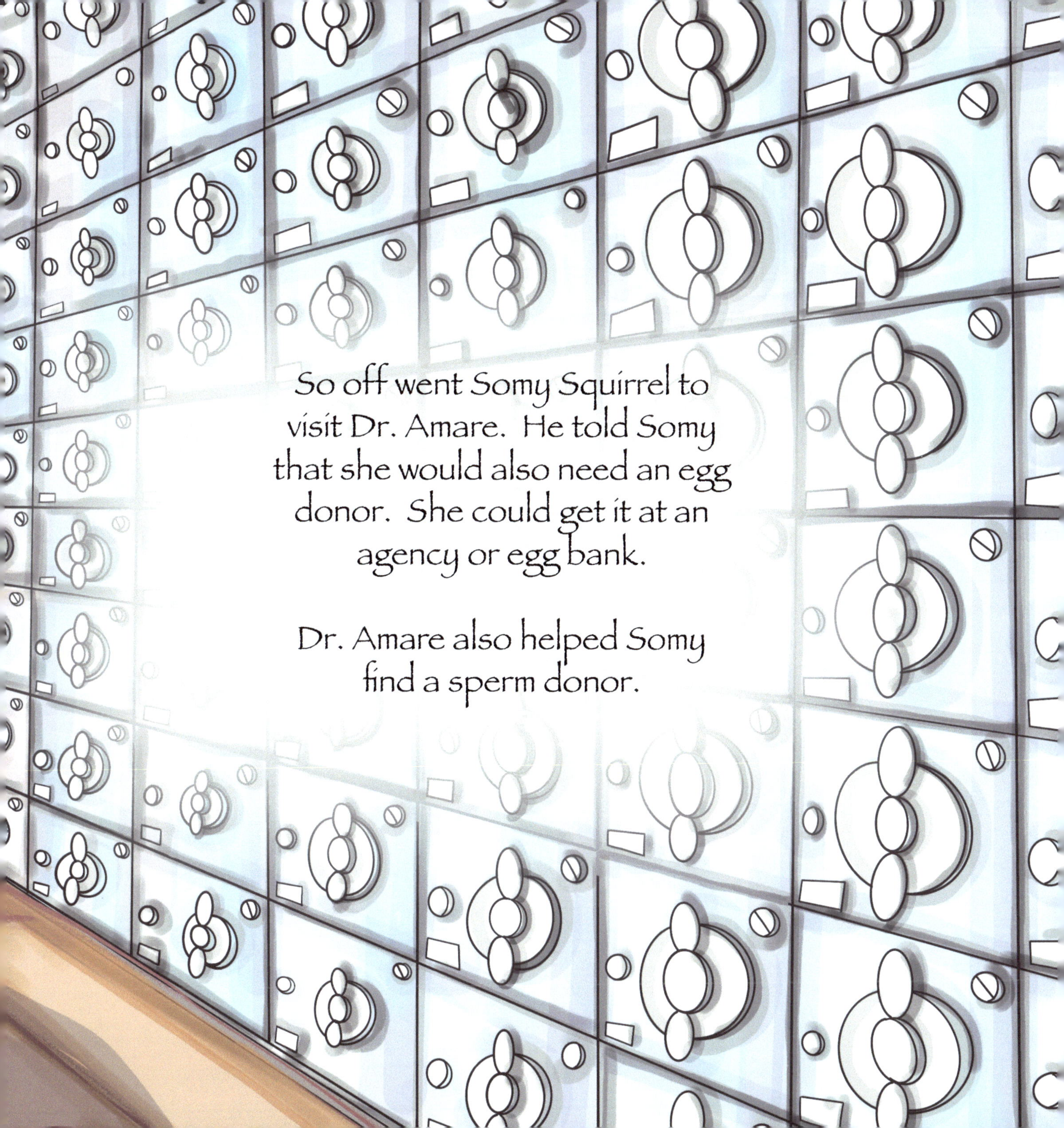

So off went Somy Squirrel to
visit Dr. Amare. He told Somy
that she would also need an egg
donor. She could get it at an
agency or egg bank.

Dr. Amare also helped Somy
find a sperm donor.

In the clinic, Dr. Amare gently put
the donated egg and the donated sperm
together in a test tube and patiently
looked after them until they fertilised
and became one, forming an embryo,
which is the beginning of a baby.

When the embryo started to grow,
Dr. Amare placed it carefully
into Somy Squirrel's womb,
where it continued…

growing… and growing…
and growing.

23

24

and then in Somy's womb,
the little baby squirrel
continued growing...
and growing...
and growing.

Somy's friends and family were so excited
about her pregnancy that they organised
a baby shower for little baby squirrel!

At last Somy
became a Mummy!

Little baby squirrel was born!
Such a beautiful and desired baby squirrel!
Together they became
a very happy family!

28

Be the heroes of your own story.

Personalise your own story with your own names.

www.fertilitybooks.net
books.carmenmartinezjover.com

EGG DONATION

A tiny itsy bitsy gift of life, an egg donor story for girls, boys and twins.

ADOPTION

Soul's time to be born, an adoption story.

SINGLE MUM BY CHOICE

Forever together, a single mum by choice story for one child or twins.

EGG AND SPERM DONATION

TWO DADS

Two tiny itsy bitsy Gifts of Life,
an egg and sperm donor story.

The baby kangaroo treasure hunt,
a gay parenting story for one child or twins.

Other books by: Rosemary & Carmen Martinez Jover

Available in:

I want to have a child, whatever it takes!

Recipes of How Babies are Made

Bloom, wherever you may be planted